HOW TO PICK YOUR BRIDE

and

HOW TO KEEP HER FOR *Life*

The Best News for *Adult Christian Males*

MICHAEL BAEZ

WESTBOW
PRESS®
A DIVISION OF THOMAS NELSON
& ZONDERVAN

WestBow Press books may be ordered through booksellers or by contacting:

WestBow Press
A Division of Thomas Nelson & Zondervan
1663 Liberty Drive
Bloomington, IN 47403
www.westbowpress.com
844-714-3454

Scripture taken from the King James Version of Bible, The New International
Reader's Version(NIrV), and The International Inductive Study Bible

First Edition

Spiritual Food Publications Corp
P.O. Box 780197
Maspeth, NY 11378-9997

ISBN: 978-1-6642-4383-5 (sc)
ISBN: 978-1-6642-4384-2 (hc)
ISBN: 978-1-6642-4382-8 (e)

Library of Congress Control Number: 2021918027

Print information available on the last page.

WestBow Press rev. date: 10/05/2021

CONTENTS

TESTIMONIES

Nivea M. says, "I finished reading your book. Have to say that I like it. The first pages brought tears to my eyes. I like the conclusion very much. Men will read it (and women also). What is good for the king is also good for the queen. Overall, I liked it, and the purpose of the book to my understanding is fulfilled; you put in it your personal life experience. Not many people are willing and able to open the veils that cover their lives. Good job!

Claudia L.—married for twenty-five years and counting—says, "*How to Pick your Bride and How to Keep Her for Life* is an insightful book that aims to build long-lasting marriages. Michael Baez's phrase "I was blind" explains his own journey of self-discovery and newfound awareness of the importance of submission to God. Throughout the book, he maintains his focus on the strong connection between biblical principles and a fruitful marriage. This book is highly recommended for couples who are seeking to restore or strengthen their marriages."

Glenn M.—a Christian husband who has been successfully married for nine years, father, real estate owner, and engineer—says, "This thought-provoking book has in-your-face calls to action and deep insights while tying in a unique biblical perspective!"

David Jennings—of the New Life Community Health Center and married for thirty-six years—says, "This is a book on relationships and marriage that was birthed out of both painful experiences and the joy of finding a new way forward. Michael offers insights into how he found hope and joy in his marriage through scripture and simple responses to life's many stressful circumstances."

Robert J.—happily married eleven years and father of two—says, "This book is straight to the point and focuses by applying biblical principles from the author's second successful marriage. The author's emphasis about being "equally yoked" is very important for a successful marriage. I recommend this book because it has taught me very important lessons about long-lasting marriages."

Kenneth B.—happily married for thirty-nine years and retired—says, "*How to Pick Your Bride and How to Keep Her for Life* is very entertaining and informative for all Christian men who are thinking about marriage or who have just gotten married. It is the perfect book to read. I am praying that the Lord will inspire the author to write another book."

Frank M. G.—married for thirty-seven years—says, "By the grace of God, I have been redeemed! My date of rebirth was August 23, 1986. The Lord has blessed me with a beautiful, loving, and Christian wife: Ana Y. She and I have been blessed with three wonderful children, one granddaughter, and one granddaughter on the way! Praise the Lord! I have come to appreciate Brother Mike Baez and his unique view of life. In his book, Mike courageously shares his own personal journey as a husband. He has clearly found his voice, and as a result, he has given a voice to many men who have been silent. May God richly bless you, Brother Mike Baez!"

Raul J. B.—a mature, devout born-again Christian, happily married husband for forty years, father of four children and four wonderful grandchildren, men's ministry leader more than a decade, small business owner, proud USMC infantry rifleman, and mortarman soldier—says, "I highly recommend brother Michael Baez's book for newly born-again in the Holy Spirit Christians who have read or are presently reading the Bible. The book is a basic tool for choosing a partner for marriage and avoiding divorce. The author's unique writing style is full of contemplative questions, references, and Bible verses. I have one negative comment: 'The book is too brief.' I am encouraging the author to write a more detailed, extensive second edition. Thank you for using your gifts to equip and bless the body or bride of Christ!"

Iñaqui M.—married for fifteen years and a proud dad—says, "The book inspires and makes me reflect through the author's personal examples and biblical truths about marriage, love, sacrifice, and the eternal goal of following Jesus Christ as our true north and compass.

Doorman Nelson M. says, "The book is very encouraging for a single guy like me who still wants to get married."

To my Father, the Living God, God Almighty, His perfect living example, my Brother, Jesus, King of Kings, and our dedicated Helper, the Holy Spirit.

Special thanks to the Word who gave me these words and to the Holy Spirit who transmitted and made these words a part of me. Thanks to mom, the first editor of my book. Thanks to my wife for making these words come alive in my life. Thanks to my close friends, Dave and Cindy Jennings, the second editors. They revealed how to form and print these words into this small yet powerful book.

AUTHOR'S NOTE

A number of men can get a woman to marry them just by saying, "I love you. Will you marry me?" This book is for Christian men who have read the Bible, which reveals God's teachings on how to get your wife to agape love you and want you for life!

The book contains two parts, and the second part emphasizes the key points found in part 1. Christian men who require more biblical evidence to apply the teachings presented this book will benefit from reading part 2. Part 1 and Part 2 are both important, but part 2 will solidify the Bible's teachings on how to stay married for life. The Bible contains much information, and studying it enough times might awaken to the fact that it often repeats vital information and concepts, creating a pattern. Many men struggle to understand all the information God wants to provide us in one sitting—let alone one lifetime. It also seems it is taking God many human lifetimes over a course of generations to get His simple point across. Those who learn and understand His teachings will be rewarded, but that is another book.

I was blind!

ABOUT THE AUTHOR

I am sinner, saved by Christ, who wishes to share the experiences and marital knowledge God has lovingly graced upon me. I have dedicated more than sixteen years of my life to working at a Christian church, and I have observed the interactions and relationships of fellow Christians. I have visited many different churches of various denominations during my travels to visit friends.

Twelve years of my early life were spent in Catholic school and Masses. For my first biblical assignment in my catechism class, I was asked to read some chapters in Genesis. After reading the whole chapter for homework, I was curious. I wanted to read Revelations to see how the book ended. The next day, eagerly wanting to discuss the homework assignment, I questioned the priest during class, revealing how I knew more than his homework assignment required. I thought I would be appreciated for going above and beyond what I had been asked to study, but he went on to scold me loudly and publicly. I was crushed and embarrassed.

Looking back, it is clear that I did not know how to relate to people from first grade through senior year. For those years, I basically felt alone, and I did not know how to make friends. I was searching, seeking, and wondering about how to relate to people and deal with this thing God created called life.

My family seemed normal, but as I got older, I realized we were not doing the things that were taught at church. My father was unable to relate to my mother, and they were always arguing. I heard the same at school: arguing. I was taught arguing, not loving, and I became pretty adept at it.

There was something else I was not taught about at home or in school: women. I was close to my mother and grandmother, and they argued often. As a result, they suffered greatly. I did not realize that I was no better than my earthly father at dealing with women. From freshman year until graduation, I struggled to find a girlfriend. My family knew how to deal with people properly, but they only applied it to their bosses, policemen, or people they were meeting for the first time. From birth through high school, I was not taught how to deal with women.

Shortly after graduating from high school, I was introduced to positive mental attitude books. These books crystallized biblical scriptures in my mind for how to find friends. I dove into the scriptures eagerly, and I spent a lot of time reading the Bible from cover to cover. After applying God's principles, I no longer had trouble making friends—but I was not yet awakened about how to marry for life.

The Lord gave me a strong, uncontrollable desire to find a wife, but I had not been taught three important lessons: understanding money, being equally yoked, and marrying for life. I married my first wife shortly after entering college. Like many people, I was not prepared. I felt I was wonderfully loving and kind to her. I tried not to treat her like I had observed other people treating each other when I was growing up.

Before reading these books, I was just like many other people. I believe my first wife loved me because I applied the scriptural references I had learned from these books. I still believe my first wife's parents also loved me. Applying biblical how-to love principles helped hide the fact that I was a non-college graduate employed as a banker at minimum wage. My wife, coming from a very successful and well-off family, did not know poverty and was disappointed with my inability to provide the lifestyle she was used to with her parents. My lack of finances did not stop me from providing her everything else a wife needs from her husband.

Lesson 1: Go to school and don't marry until you earn enough money to take care of your family.

Read the scripture on how God instructed newlyweds to build their farms before their houses:

> Prepare thy work without, and make it fit for thy self in the field, and afterward build thine house. (Proverbs 24:27 King James Version of Bible)

Alert to my wife's need for wealthier experiences, I complained to the Lord in prayer: "Why is this happening? I am going to a Baptist church and have been extremely loving to my wife." My earthly father graduated high school and was able to take care of a family of four and others.

The Holy Spirit came and filled my mind with knowledge about marriage. This book is not me; I was strenuously compelled by the Holy Spirit to write, at times not even sleeping at night. I spent about two years of my life working at my minimum-wage job, loving my wife (applying the principles the Holy Spirit sent me), and writing the words the Lord gave me about how to marry for life.

Thanks to God, the book was finally finished. I knew there was a possibility that I could provide for my first wife's financial needs. However, shortly after I finished the book, my first wife moved out of my presence. Again, I complained to the Lord: "I did everything you told me in the book!" I was willing to go with her to counseling, but shortly thereafter, she was gone without any contact. She was many states away from my home. I wanted to marry her for life! It was then that I realized the book was not yet complete.

Struggling and stressed with near minimum-wage income for six months, not knowing any better, I began searching for another wife. I decided I would look for a more mature woman. I applied all the principles I had learned from God—everything I believe the Father had told me—but I avoided the *equally yoked* lessons of the Bible. My first wife had only been two years older than me, and I felt the need to find a more mature woman. My second wife was sixteen years older than me. After applying the other principles of the book the Holy Spirit gave me, she decided to marry me.

Still recovering from a feeling of abandonment, my first wife returned. She wanted to reengage the marriage. God knew I was applying what He had taught me in the book, but I did not think my first wife would be a prodigal. By that time, I was going to have my first child with my second wife, and I chose to send my first wife away.

I included the prodigal knowledge in the book and lived the book with my second wife. Equally yoked lessons were lightly applied to my second wife, but I regretted not applying it more strongly as I explained in my book. It might have improved my married life a hundredfold. Being equally yoked is a very important lesson from the Bible.

I did not strongly apply the equally yoked principle, but I did apply other biblical skills from the book. This book will be helpful for young men who are not married but of marrying age or married men who are struggling in their marriages. Experienced husbands will find tips for how to reinforce their marriages the way Jesus does. It will also be good for churches with high divorce rates.

Marriage can be fun and fulfilling, but many singles don't know that it takes a lot of work. Are you prepared? It takes a man who is willing to apply the God-given principles found in the Bible about marriage. Marriage to my second wife was not easy, but applying and living the principles in my book made it many times easier. My wife and I had wonderful moments and experiences together. Arguments were kept to a minimum, and they were certainly not like I experienced as a child.

Thankfully, the Lord gave me the knowledge to *restart*. It worked when I was at fault and needed to change. It even worked when my wife was at fault. Twice in my second marriage, we had arguments— and my wife threatened to divorce me. My wife forgot about divorce within a day after I applied what I learned from this book.

This book taught me how to love my wife the way the Father and

Jesus love my wife and me. If the Father is willing to apply His love to me, I am willing and happy to apply it to my wife. In a miraculous way, lovingly applying this knowledge successfully kept me married to my second wife for thirty-four years. We had wonderful times loving, traveling, volunteering, spending time in church, and enjoying contemporary Christian concerts. She is responsible for giving me a wonderful daughter who is now married.

My wife is a wonderful woman—alive in Christ as of March 1, 2020, due to cancer—and I miss her greatly. I look forward to loving her again when I am with the Lord.

PART 1

The Words the Father Made Me Document via the Holy Spirit

A WORD ABOUT THE BIBLE

The Bible is an autobiography about the one true God. It is the true story of God and His battle for equal attention and love. The Bible is an instruction manual; it provides complete instructions for living. It is also a great political textbook, revealing examples of actual government rules and regulations. It contains the records of political leaders and their great examples and failures. It teaches political leaders how to woo the hearts of the people. It teaches how to be a leader. Much information is laid out in kingdom after kingdom. It explains true correctness (righteousness), the future, and much more. The book also contains the true historical record, and it provides access to unbeatable tactics of war. The Old Testament and the New Testament help believers in their everyday lives.

God's book teaches everything you need to know about sex. The concepts of property and value are thoroughly explained. It provides readers with all the information they need to understand life and themselves.

Are you interested in advanced programming? It is in there. It is the most complete textbook humans will ever find! Not the textbook type? Would you enjoy reading the world's greatest romance novel? The Bible is the best-selling book in the world. I pray for the people who are literally dying for a copy. God's great book is the ultimate guide to love, fulfillment, marriage, and completeness. Do you have one? Have you used it yet?

WHAT GOD WANTS

Your purpose is what God wants most of all! Ever wonder why God created us? Is loneliness a godlike feeling? When God created the earth, the Bible reveals His ownership of many beings. My personal conclusion is He wants a wife!

If God had a choice of a thousand wives, I am sure He would pick the best. If He had only one choice, would He take whomever He could get?

Biblical fact? God has no one to select. The solution is that no wife exists for God; therefore, He has to create. Create is an important word. How should you feel when you create something? God feels glorious!

Understanding and perfecting your purpose will help your marriage.

ABOUT GOD'S WIFE

When you create something, should it be perfect? God wants His creations to be perfect. It has to be perfect to bring Him glory. I can't think of anything human beings create where glory is not important. Hand a child a box of crayons and paper to work on, and upon completion of the creation—maybe a creation truly fit for the garbage—the child begs for approval and glory. What do authors do when their creations are not perfect?

What type of wife does God want? A perfect wife. What is a perfect wife? Willfully submissive and obedient. Submissive in what way? God has the final say. The best biblical example of this is Jesus and what he said in Luke 22:42.

What glory is there in getting submission or obedience if it is not earned? Where is the glory in receiving glory if the being you get it from is less of a being than you are? What if she is less in wisdom, less in strength, less in knowledge, or less in ability? Do we search for fellowship with amoebas?

All sports lovers enjoy winning, but where is the glory if you beat a bad team? God's ultimate wife must be equal. Equal is important for interaction. If the important thing in your life is to have your wife with you when you jog your twenty miles per day, there is a problem if your wife only jogs two miles per day. Are mental and physical things important?

God's ultimate wife must be willfully submissive and obedient, godlike, and equal in knowledge, strength, power, and ability.

GOD'S GIFT TO ADAM

G od's most advanced godlike creations were human—men *and* women. Weaker than God, humans were created to have the most forward understanding of God. Truly capable of godlike thinking, humans are not currently capable of complete interaction with God.

Adam was so godlike before his fall that he wanted what God wanted. God gave Adam what Adam wanted before God could get what He wanted. The perfect solution was Eve. Eve was virtually equal both physically and mentally to Adam. She needed to submit to God and Adam, but God decided to include free will!

THE PROBLEM OF THE MILLENNIUM

How do you find a bride who is equal in power, wisdom, knowledge, and ability—and who is willing to submit and be obedient?

If women wanted to be like men, the most macho qualities they could imitate are submissiveness and obedience. A great example of machismo is King David. He was a giant fighter and a warrior. Do you know who he is submissive and obedient to?

Your most important purpose in life is deciding if you want to get married. Before you say no to the proposal, you should look at the potential husband you are turning away. If you decide to get married, should you learn about the husband you are marrying? Should learning include knowledge of His ways and thoughts?

CREATIONS OUT OF ORDER

I f you marry, what do you get? You get the living room. You get to enjoy interesting conversation. If you are tired, you have a place to rest. You could sit in the den, read a good book, walk in the garden, take a dip in the pool, step in the kitchen, turn on the radio, watch TV, and go out the front door. If you don't marry God, what is He to do with you? What do you do with your creations that are not perfect or useful? Throw them in the garbage? I don't think God has the heart to throw away any of His godlike creations. Do you have any creations of your own gathering dust on the shelf? What about in the basement? In the attic? In the closet? God believes that one equal and submissive partner will satisfy the want.

How does God feel about same-sex marriages? Adultery against God? What is He going to do about it? Read Proverbs 6:32–35.

HUMAN MALE CREATIONS

Why are you lost in pornographic and non-pornographic pictures, movies, and TV shows? Have you tried touching them? Do they feel like one of God's fine creations? Do the people in these shows ever listen to what you have to say? What about harlots? She will not satisfy your built-in wants unless she is willing to marry you for life.

Can you have a relationship with a camel load of gold? Do you tend to throw away or hoard a lot of the materials you buy? Do you know why? Why not marry your dream girl and head toward the straight-and-narrow path?

It is the path toward completion.

HOW TO PICK YOUR WIFE AND STAY MARRIED FOR LIFE!

Y ou need a place to start. Start here. Picture in your mind your bride. What does she look like? If it's not desirable, pick another. Very important point. Decide what you have to offer your dream girl. What are you willing to give?

If your dream girl wants less, great. Give it all to her! If your dream girl wants it all, fantastic. What will you do if your dream girl wants more? If she marries you, she will expect it for life. No divorce.

Find her. She must be equal, submissive, and obedient. An important detail: The more equal your dream girl is, the harder she will be to find. Is she out there?

Experience her, understand her, and seek out her wants. Can you afford her? Do you want her? A little tap dance is OK. It is what you have to give. If you both decide to go steady, this is my secret weapon. Ask her how you make her feel. Make her put it in writing. It is your scorecard.

In marriage, many couples say I do and never know what that means. Some husbands may know their wives are happy or angry, but they never know how their brides feel about them. Getting a written list when you have recently started dating—or at least recently gotten married—tells you what your date or wife thinks about you. It is very informative and can be like a keel in the marriage. She may be willing to write this list if you write her a long love letter first to let her know all the wonderful reasons why you have chosen her.

Once you are sure she has read and understood your letter, ask her to write a note telling you why she wants to be with you. At a later time, in the marriage—possibly after a serious argument—ask her the question again. It can reveal where you have gone wrong, and you can possibly do something about it instead of misunderstanding her actions.

Some things can't be changed, but many things can. What is wrong? You don't know until you have asked her to write down your scorecard and then ask her to write it again as you feel you need to. I asked my wife, who is now deceased, that question twice in our lifetime together. You may have to ask more.

Are you satisfied with your scorecard? Are there any other feelings she wants to feel? Does she want to be a star? Pick her up and sit her in front of the TV. Watch her—and refuse to change channels! Admire her—and tell her what you enjoy about her. Actions speak louder than words! Use both!

Is there something you absolutely cannot give her? Tell her you can't (macho brain battle)! Next, present her with as many logical reasons you are willing to think of why you cannot give her that something. Did you win the battle? Feminine tears? Was the argument worth it?

Winning the battle is sometimes necessary, but it is not always worth the argument. You know how it feels. Men, women, and children often have resentments even though they are righteously corrected. Too much unnecessary correction can have a detrimental effect on a marriage. While children seem to be flexible, adults seem to get more rigid as they get older. They are not as recuperative, and they are more vengeful and stressed out. Pick your battles wisely. While this stress may be necessary at the workplace, you have to decide if the argument is worth it in your home or when you are together. If the argument is worth it, follow through, over, under, around, and through it. Be the first to restart your affections by the next day—even if she is still upset with you for doing the right thing. You might have to start from the beginning. Do you understand?

Love her. Give to her. Want her. This is what will bring her to life!

Is she an introvert with no confidence? Be patient. Is she an extrovert and confident? Be patient. Work harder. She must understand that you want her more than anyone else. Don't worry about money. You want to give her what she wants, but she does not know what she wants! Do you know what she wants?

Build up those *love bucks,* the currency of the future, through acts of love, gifts of love, loving experiences, loving words, loving help, loving attention, and by knowing what she likes and loves. The second commandment tells us to love your neighbor as yourself.

Do you know who the printer of those love bucks is? Do you understand the transaction? Build up those love bucks! Have you been building? How hard are you building? How much effort are you putting in? Don't be concerned about receiving a return on your love bucks so soon!

Many married men are told marriage is a fifty-fifty proposition. It is Christlike to consider it is 100 percent. Don't be in a rush to immediately get your 100 percent return on the love bucks you spend on your bride. It is Christlike to make a strong, consistent effort to give her your 100 percent. It is great to offer as much credit as possible concerning the love you give your wife.

Is there something you want? Check your Bible. The Father never asked—and neither did the Son. Ask her! Was her answer no? What nerve! Be patient. Save what you truly want for the end. If you get it, you have won. Be careful. Enjoy it.

Do you really want it? Read on. How long must you endure this effort you put in to getting what you want? The answer is as long as you want to. But you have been struggling with her for years. Do you want to start over? Ha!

Should you wait until she gives up? Should you wait until she is alive? Do you have her attention? How does she feel when she is with you? Is she on the hook? Is her attention divided?

Don't worry. Build up those love bucks! I know it hurts. Do you understand now? When should you give up? When you feel godlike? When you feel like a man? When you feel like a woman? When you feel like a child? How about when you feel lower than a tomato?

It happened to me. Does she want you? Have you waited long enough?

Jesus would never do the following:

- Put Himself first: If you have grown impatient, yell about how you feel! When many men marry, they feel like they have a right to force-feed negative feelings about their spouse any time and all the time. It must be carefully understood and agreed to with the spending of much love bucks.
- Jesus would never give up on you or your relationship. He has not complained to me when I was wrong. Has he personally complained to you in a negative way? If you have consistently been building love bucks, like Jesus would—and you think her love for you is true but you are not sure—tell her what *you* want. Even if you are choosing what you want wisely, this request could possibly be the end of the relationship (omega). Instead, offer to go with her to a Christian counselor. Find an intermediary. If she leaves, will you wait for her return (Luke 15:11–24)?

If she stays, will you be happy? Do you understand what you want? The best biblical example is one I heard a pastor preach one Sunday. Jesus was praying at the Garden of Gethsemane. He had the disciples nearby. The disciples were his chosen family of dedicated followers. When the soldiers came to arrest Jesus, His disciples and close friends—who Jesus treated as brothers—offered no assistance and scattered. Jesus was beaten until He was unrecognizable, and He died on the cross. When Jesus rose from the dead and returned to the apostles, He did not yell in anger or say "Where were you when I was beaten? You abandoned me! I thought you would back me up." After proving that he was alive, Jesus, the King of the world, appeared to some disciples—not in anger, frustration, vengeance, or to complain—as a servant making breakfast.

The Father and Jesus seem to be teaching us to continuously spend our love bucks until the end. If your bride realizes that you have persistently been spending your love bucks on her the way Jesus would and you have a moment where you can no longer be Christlike, tell her what you are feeling and tell her what you want. If she does not know how to express her love back to you, but you get what you want, it will reveal to you that she loves you and wants you. Use your newfound understanding and power sparsely and wisely and continue spending those love bucks on her.

Timing is very important here. Give it a lot of time before you ask her what you want. It would be better to be Christlike, depending on the Lord's rewards, and not ask.

GIVE IT SOME TIME

Have you been super good to her? My first wedding was glorious, but it cost me dearly. It was a combination of love and fights. She left me for a better job. I wept for a year. I wanted her for life!

A year later, she called me back and said, "I want you."

By that time, I had picked someone else. Will your bride be a prodigal? If you want her and have been good to her as Christ would have been and she still leaves, I recommend waiting two years before going on to seek another.

More love and less fighting is critical to a relationship.

What does your bride want?

- She wants what God wants!
- She wants what the female should want.
- She wants what all men want.
- She wants what all parents want.
- She wants what all children want.
- She wants what all newborns want.
- She wants to be wanted.

When a baby is born, the parents should be extremely enthusiastic about the child. The baby could not care less about the parents because another set of loving parents will do adequately. What must you do about it? There has to be a time before the child decides to turn off when the child realizes that you *want* the child.

Is the light of your child turned off? Try turning the child on. Toys are not important. Time with parents for playing and learning is important and helps the child realize that their parents want them. I believe a child's access to parents is important and must be reinforced often.

We are all born with the want to be wanted. It is a God-created program. It is a very important part of what makes us godlike, and it is necessary for *true life*. Some people are not truly alive.

Babies show they need to be wanted when they request to be changed, fed, or held. Children show it when they want attention. Adults demonstrate it through their greetings. Wanting things from other people demonstrates the need to be wanted, but it does not necessarily satisfy the need to be wanted.

Some children give the appearance of no longer wanting to be wanted before eighteen, and others seem to lose their desire to want to be wanted when they start dealing with the world after eighteen. Some people channel it into the work they do, and they may be satisfied as long as their work survives.

Christians are retaught the program in its true God-intended form when they attach themselves to Christ and work toward being Christlike. It is only then that you can live a true life. God and marriage are meant to be the fulfillment of the program. The need to be wanted is the same as wanting to be loved.

GIVE HER THE GIFTS YOU
WERE BORN WITH

What does your dream girl want? Could it be everything you have? Have you forgotten the gifts you were born with?

- eyes to look at her
- ears to listen to her (most important)
- mouth to communicate (how much you want her)
- your touch
- your attention

These core wants were made by our Creator. If you want her for life, she will want to be your wife. She may not understand what is going on, but she will have a hard time resisting properly applied godlike, Christlike attention.

GOD ALSO WANTS

What does God want? He wants you! Your godlike attention is requested. He wants you to get to know Him and His ways through fellowship and prayer. He wants you perfect—so accept Jesus Christ as your Savior. Apply His teachings and awaken. If necessary, Christ will awaken you (ouch!).

The Ten Commandments? How about the suggestions? Ignore them at your own peril. Better still, consider them as what you want. It is built in. Jesus Christ is the way to completion!

God has been trying to tell people, tribes, and nations what they want for many thousands of years. People have formed failed relationship after failed relationship. Try counting the number of times He was divorced and turned down.

IS GOD ANGRY?

"I will not submit to an angry God!" Read about the chosen people. God pursues the chosen people like a husband. God will redeem His Chosen people (Hosea 1–3). Jesus was also in pursuit mode when He said He would marry His church. Look at the attention God has given to them.

When you understand the scriptures, you understand the great preparation God did before creation, during creation, and after the creation of this universe. He has done everything a male is supposed to do in preparation for marriage, including choosing a bride. Notice how Jesus imitates the Father in preparation, pursuit mode, in choosing, and in the godly question He asked. These examples from the Bible are simplified and explained in this book. These biblical examples reveal how to find and hold onto your bride.

I am against any physical violence or punishment toward your bride, but Romans 12:19 King James Version of Bible says, "Vengeance is mine," saith the Lord. God, as Father, has to punish you when you are disobedient. O, how the chosen people have been punished!

God should be angry! Why? Read the questions Moses asked God (Numbers 11:11–20). The reading is a good example of the questions the chosen people asked God. You have read the Bible. You have read the good books on sales. You may have had a wife. You have had parents. Why didn't Moses or the chosen people ask God how He feels?

- What do you say to God when you pray?
- How does God feel about the poor?
- How does God feel about slaves?
- How does God feel about the sick?

Read the Old Testament and see what our Father has done for the chosen people, all people. Read the New Testament and see what our Father has done for the chosen people, all people.

Can a maid forget her ornaments, or a bride her attire? Yet My people have forgotten Me days without number. (Jeremiah 2:32 King James Version of Bible)

Our Father's patience is at an end. Did you count the number of times God was disregarded in the Old Testament? So much for second chances.

Thank God He sent us His Son, Jesus Christ. Jesus is now running the show, giving the Father a break (Matthew 28:18), and He will not accept any animal sacrifices.

- How many chances has Jesus given you?
- There is an end to His patience.
- How does it relate to marriage?

If you have read the Old Testament and the New Testament thoroughly, you understand. First, Jesus's patience is not at the end yet. God has repeatedly been mistreated, ignored, and disposed of by His future Bride after providing so much, but He is still showing love by feeding the wheat and the tares?

What mistreatment by your bride have you put up with?

He is still pursuing you and all of us from the beginning to the end. Through the ups and the downs, from your rebellion to your acceptance, from your hate to your love, His provision is nonstop. His pursuit is continuous, His listening is all ears, His effort not stopping, and His love does not want to end. If you are married to God, would you accept anything less? If you are a pursuing male choosing to marry, do you think your bride would appreciate anything less? Do you feel Jesus is providing the perfect example of how to love your bride? Is there a godly lesson here about how you should love your bride?

EQUALLY YOKED

I n the Bible, two oxen were held together by a yoke, which hinted at the problems the farmer would have plowing his fields if the oxen on the yoke were imbalanced. Church teachers preach about the need to have the same denomination to balance a marriage.

If you are searching for a wife, being equally yoked means more than being in the same denomination. Though it is no excuse for divorce, there is a need to know how equal both of you are before you marry—unless you plan to be argumentative for life. Will you be willing to compromise?

What is important to you? What is important to her?

Throughout this book, there are hints about being equally yoked. Other important equals to consider include :

- Your faith, obedience to God, following the same books that give you godly instruction, and agreeing upon the same instructor of those books. It will solve much debate.
- Intimacy, child, and child-rearing plans and techniques.
- Goals for family income.
- Expense desires and saving desires (what you want to spend money on).
- Activities, interests, and how you plan to spend your time together.
- Culture equalities and inequalities.
- Conditions you are willing to live in. Are you equal?

- Dreams and expectations.
- What do you want? What does she want?
- Flexibility. Are you really flexible?
- Do you want to be wanted? Does she want to be wanted?

The list could go on and on. The bigger the foundation you agree upon, the fewer stressful debates you will have. Marriage will give you enough things to discuss. Build and check the balance of your yoke before marriage.

HAVE YOU PICKED
A BRIDE YET?

Christian, what is your problem? What is your problem? Place an advertisement in bold print that says "I want a bride!" A Christian bride is preferred when both of you utilize the Bible as your final court of arbitration. When those ladies line up, pick one. Is she not perfect? Are you not sure?

Carefully look at her from head to toe, one square inch at a time. Ask her to talk. Do you like her voice? If you like a part, you must take the whole. Don't forget to turn her around. Still not sure? Offer her a seat. Grab a pen and a pad and ask questions. Write them down. Probe her mind. Understand her heart. Is she not perfect? Problem? Can you not fix her? Fix yourself first.

Is she a person who wants to be wanted? Still not sure? Put her on a stage and ask her to tap dance. Seek the wonders she can do! Search for equalities!

- Is she not perfect? Will you marry her?
- Do you truly need to pick another?
- Do you understand?

Marry her. Why wait until Jesus comes? Maybe you will get a small taste of paradise on this evil planet. If not, your Christlike efforts will be rewarded in heaven.

In many marriages, no true assessment is done when the bride is chosen. This book encourages the man pursuing a bride to know what he wants in a bride before the heat of the moment kicks in. Assessment should not be just physical; it should be mental too. Make a strong attempt to understand her heart. Equality seems to be worth searching for. Know what you want in as many aspects as possible and what you are willing to give up.

At the same time, this book is very powerful. A Christlike person puts many people at ease with less need for arguments, making people more willing to change from their sinful, selfish natures. The sinful nature of a person may be easier to correct by learning and adopting a more Christlike nature, which is taught in the Bible and this book, but it is recommended that the husband change himself first. Know where you can be more flexible. Know what you are willing not to seek or argue about.

Choose what you want and what you want to argue about wisely.

THE ANSWER IS LOVE

If you believe it is better not to touch a woman and better to marry Christ, put a gold ring on your finger and consider yourself married for life. This is a command from heaven.

- Are you searching?
- I want love. It is a commandment, and it is an order. Wake up!
- I will get it. Why? Because I can give it.
- Do you understand?
- Show me!
- Without me, you will be incomplete.
- You will never understand!
- Do you want to be on automatic pilot?
- Awaken and see the light!
- Do you like programming?

Our Father and Jesus live those words. It will be great for your marriage when you become confident enough to live the above words for your bride. This is how you wake her up. Your bride will be alive when she can live those words for you.

Learn from the Programmer!

In this was manifested the love of God toward us, because that God sent his only begotten Son into the

world, that we might live through him. (1 John 4:9
King James Version of Bible)

How does it relate to marriage? "Living through Him" defines restitution to God for our sins and is an example to imitate so we can learn how to live.

Our Father is the Programmer. He designed our bodies, souls, and hearts. In the Bible, you can read how He is prepping for a wedding. If you understand the Old Testament, you can see that the snake caused Adam and Eve to fall into sin. You can also read about all the steps the Programmer made to reprogram our fallen selves and prepare us for a bond as close as marriage.

Jesus provides a second biblical example of how you can change hearts—your heart and her heart—in preparation for marriage. It is good to learn from them to know how to marry for life and to set an example for your bride.

ABOUT THE WORD WANT

Love equals want. Agape love equals agape want. Heaven is the place where you will be wanted. Hell is the horrible place where you won't be wanted. Want is a key word. Do you know what you want?

KNOW YOUR PURPOSE

To Love God, you must join the living and ask God what He wants.

Ask your bride what she wants. Repeatedly ask your bride the godly and biblical question: What do you want? Do this in an effort to raise her from the dead. You can tell if she is fully awake if she seriously and repeatedly asks you, "What do you want?"

It's important to pray!

PRAYER

Lord God, how are you feeling today? I praise you, want you, and need you. Please face the people of the world and fix their hearts, their souls, and their physical bodies.

Is there anything you want from me today?

Add your prayer here:

MARRIAGE COVENANT VOWS

Believing that people no longer understand traditional marriage vows, I wrote a marriage covenant for the bride and groom to recite, which I believe is biblical and easier to understand:

> I accept, want, and need Jesus Christ as my Lord and Savior. I will obey Him forever. I want (Name)_____ as my bride/groom for life and will for life make you feel wanted according to God's definition of love as written in His book.

> For the rest of my life, I will give you my eyes, ears, touch, and attention. I am burning with passion. Your thoughts, words, feelings, and wants are and will be important to me. Please give me your mind, heart, and body to possess and own. I humbly request the Father, the Son, and the Holy Spirit to seal my want and remove my free will. I want God's gift of eternal joy, and in return, starting now, I willfully give Him my eternal love. I will love you for life!

LOVE WITH PASSION!

The apostle Paul hints that burning with passion is the only reason to marry (1 Corinthians 7:9). I believe there is a need for celibacy within the church, but an additional reason for marriage is the same as it always was. Loneliness is what started all life, and it is a worthwhile reason to marry.

The Bible shows how when loneliness is ended with marriage, the resulting love should include passion. Some of us want passion, and some of us don't want passion. I believe the reason why some want and some do not to want is to continue the godly celibate examples that offer future generations an opportunity to figure out the patterns of God's life when compared to the Messiah's life. Our choice examples are the Creator and the Messiah. Consider their patience. You can imitate their lives as written in the scriptures, which includes celibacy, or follow their orders and marry with love for your wife for life without divorce.

If you are burning with passion on earth, it will be worth your while to marry a bride who also is burning with passion. Searching for such equality is different than searching for physical or mental equals. Material things will not enter paradise. God's prime directive is creating human couples, one male and one female, who will love each other passionately. Once married, passion will be the hardest lesson in the Bible to teach your bride.

If the woman you want to be your bride refuses to use the included marriage covenant, I would seriously question her reason for marriage and consider choosing another bride. The covenant works both ways and should be recited by husband and wife. When both you and your bride are burning with passion, as God's book recommends, marital arguments should decrease.

If you were made with no passion and choose to marry, it would be worth your time to find a similar bride. Be prepared if your bride demands more attention. It is better to marry when you are burning with passion.

Taking the time to let her experience your Christlike self while you get to know her is the best way to open her heart to how important you feel this matter is. Being equally yoked before marriage may be important here. The men who want passion (who marry brides with no passion), including those men who don't want passion (who marry brides who want passion) can expect to have arguments from the beginning of their wedding day.

For those who are already married, the Bible is a passionate book. Those who did not receive their passion programs will find them if they seek them out. If you expect the woman you have married to love you with passion, expect to apply much Christlike love. Christlike love includes Christlike attention year after year.

If you are already married, and your marriage needs love to be defined, you can renew your marriage vows using the included marriage covenant in this book. Complete love is defined in the Bible and is what God wants. Complete love is more easily discussed with a Christian wife after applying much Christlike love. The longer your wife has studied her Bible—and the more experienced your Christlike love—the more likely she will respond when the scriptures are taught.

YOU MUST BE BORN AGAIN!

I t doesn't mean going back inside your mother. Jesus was talking about the perfect state you were in when you came out! It means wanting to be wanted so Jesus Christ can come into your life and then give you to our Father.

Jesus wants the change in your heart. He wants the change in your heart to go back to the way you were when you were born. You might not remember the attention you gave to your mother or father. How you always wanted to look at them. How you were persistently listening to them. How you always wanted to hold them. How you always wanted to be with them. How you depended on them. How you loved them. You had a true living bonding need the Father programmed into you to be an example to the world.

You might not know how long your perfect state of heart lasted after you were born. It might not have lasted long because original sin is in the world you are born into. Sneaking in through the senses, mostly through the eyes and ears, original sin is passed from generation to generation. It may have changed your heart. Jesus wants you to be born again—with that bonded loving relationship state of heart—for Him and our Father to accept you.

Your bride might not admit it, but she—and we all—want that too. Yes, sometimes she may need her space, but she wants you to always be ready to return to that state of heart. Objects, animals, robots, two-dimensional talking pictures, ever-present video images, and distant voices, sounds through the air or wires will not do. Your presence, your loving touch, your eyes, your ears, and your born-again heart are what she wants. A real husband, alive and knowing how to love, is what your bride wants in a marriage. If you don't know how yet, run to, search, seek, learn, and ask the only three beings that are alive in all existence: Our Father, His Son, and the Holy Spirit

Don't act dead with your bride. Persistently show her and our Father that you are alive!

Note

Successful application of the information in this book also requires consistent prayer before marriage and persistent prayer to God after marriage. It would have helped my marriage a lot if I had been taught to pray with my wife. My personal, no-contest choices to seek out when praying by name are:

- The Great, the Mighty God Jehovah of hosts (Jeremiah 32:18–20)
- Soon-to-be King Jehovah, Our Righteousness
- God Almighty, name included because in this name, three major religions are united

AUTHOR'S FAVORITE
BIBLICAL PERSONS

Females

In Genesis

Eve

S he was the first to submit to our Father after the fall, and although undocumented, she was also the first human to attempt to love after the fall. Our Father's covenant to Eve resulted in women loving men. Genesis shows the love to have survived generations beyond the Flood and passed to Mary, the Mother of Jesus.

Sarah and Hagar

These women, committed to our Father's covenant with Eve and all women, are shown in dispute, resulting from their efforts to please Abraham. At that time, God-fearing Abraham was God's best choice for women worldwide.

Sarah's struggle to satisfy and please her husband is documented in Genesis. Her effort to feel wanted by seeking to understand and trying to please her husband is the first one documented in the Bible. Did she ask her husband the godly question: "What do you want?"

Hagar, obedient to God, is the second woman documented in the

Bible who is shown to be ready to please Abraham. The scriptures show Abraham on the right hand of God and having much favor. He was stumped by two women requiring God's intervention.

God's solution was to offer nearly the same to both wives. Such intervention was out of love for His female creations. If you believe the scriptures, Hagar became the second wife of Abraham—even though God made it easier for Abraham to deal with the problem by telling Abraham to listen only to Sarah (Genesis 21:12). May all three be at peace with our Father.

Hannah

This is another Bible-documented struggle by a wife attempting to please and feel wanted by her husband (1 Samuel 1–2).

God's chosen women in Egypt are God's favorite women. This is an eternal example. Did the mothers die? Did they die for love? Check Exodus 1:15–22.

In the New Testament (Matthew, Mark, Luke, John, and Acts)

Mary, Mother of Jesus

She continues to be part of the first blood covenant the Father made with Eve when He sacrificed a lamb after Adam and Eve were removed from the Garden of Eden. The leadership example Mary provides to us all is to submit to God and obey His command to love and serve.

These confident women set the example in marriage by searching for what God wants and what their grooms wanted. They took care of the needs of their husbands and children. These women also set an example for the men reading this book. The godly question was often on their hearts.

Males

The following men are responsible for accomplishing much in the Bible and the world we live in. Many readers already know and believe that some of them are responsible for everything in existence. The gifts, the education, the love, the attention, the example, the hope, the peace, and the understanding they provide are beyond the scope of this book. The most important thing they provide is repairing the human heart after the fall. The Bible reveals how they have worked hard to be the example and teach all humans to love and serve one another. Their willingness to seek out the wants and needs of others and provide for them shows they were the creators and/or users of the godly question: "What do you want?"

In the Old Testament and the New Testament

God Almighty

The known God of Israel by those who love Him and/or fear Him. He is the Creator, and He is the Creator of truth, beauty, all existence, and you. He is spoken about throughout this book.

In the Old Testament

Enoch

The man God brought to heaven (Genesis 5:24),

Noah

Carrier of God's Spirit and much knowledge (Genesis 5:10),

Israel's Son Joseph

He represents our Father's successful turnaround of evil in Genesis. Joseph, despite possibly frustrating his brothers and experiencing his personal tragedy, loves God, his wife, and his children. Like God, scripture shows Joseph remaining present to assist and help women during the birth of their children (Genesis 50:23 The International Inductive Study Bible New Ameican Standard Bible). The story of Joseph can be found in any Bible (Genesis 37–50).

King David

He knew how to love God, and he chose our Father's goodness and mercy—even when his nation was surrounded by evil.

King Solomon

He demonstrated to the world the importance of women as property that is most worth owning.

In the Old and New Testament

Jesus

Greater than Solomon, He accomplishes the perfect example of showing the straight-and-narrow path to paradise. He fulfills God's covenant to Eve. Women after God's work are now in demand. Jesus—the Messiah and son of Mary, during His lifetime, changed the Mosaic Law, making women and men equal property. Men could no longer divorce women at will. Marriage became binding due to our Father's efforts and His Son's efforts. Marriage now results in the man and the woman being the property of each other. The once unequal purchase value, Jesus made equal. What God has put together let no man separate (the meaning of life!). Jesus is definitely an expert where it concerns women. He is second only to our Father.

Note: Free will results in good or evil. Choose good! It can't be made any easier!

PART II

Though this book can be a quick and easy read, it contains lots of key biblical information. It also contains many words to think about and should not be read too quickly. Some words have more spaces between them in hopes that the reader takes the time to contemplate what has been written.

It is the author's hope for men to reach deep inside themselves and find the original God-programmed love that is meant for the woman God created for him. Original sin, heavy workloads, lack of forgiveness, and the added stresses of life can be some of the important Bible-revealed reasons for the loss of the definition of love in our hearts (Genesis 5:29). We all understand love when we are born, but experiencing sin after we are in the world takes away our God-programmed understanding of love. The Bible shows the primary problem after the fall to be men.

Part 2 reveals the scriptures that show how God is rebuilding His God-programmed love after the fall of Adam. It's His answer to the question, "What is love?"

Genesis 3:15 shows God taking the side of women. Eve and many women after her chose God's way. After the Flood, the Bible shows women being fully aware of the fight for love.

Genesis 16:5 shows Sarai (later known as Sarah) being wrong in her decision yet confident enough in her love to Abraham to say, "The Lord Judge between me and thee (Abraham)." God measures action and our thoughts to find out if we love Him and the gifts He gives us.

The previous scripture shows a woman who is knowledgeable of the biblical need for complete love.

Seth lived 105 years then begat Enos.
—Genesis 5:6 King James Version of Bible

Love potions not working yet?

Jesus said, "Moses because of the hardness of your hearts, suffered you to put away your wives: but from the beginning it was not so."
—Matthew 19:8 King James Version of Bible

The scripture verifies God's original intentions for men and women. From the beginning, Adam had one wife and no choice. Before the Flood, when God started over, Noah had one wife. Noah's three sons each had only one wife. The previous biblical examples including the Messiah's change in the Law explain God's will for marriage.

For this cause shall a man leave his father and mother, and shall be joined unto his wife, and they two shall be one flesh.
—Ephesians 5:31 King James Version of Bible

How to Pick Your Bride and How to Keep Her for Life   57

Another word about restarting.

If you have been doing everything biblical in your marriage, have been consistently building love bucks, and have honestly assessed that the cause of the argument is not your fault, you can decide if you want to apologize. I highly recommend restarting.

Some brothers in Christ don't have a clue about how to treat their brides. I recommend apologizing. Before restarting, do a self-assessment or have another brother in Christ assess you. Take the log out of your own eye and fix yourself. It is not your fault; no person took us aside when we were young and taught us how to marry. Be the male and carefully do what God does: restart.

You have to go backward—maybe even back to the beginning. Remember the way you were when you met her and chose to pursue her? How did you act? She liked you once—before. You were a buffoon—now change. You may have to start (not forcing, expecting, or demanding) with hello, acquaintance, true heartfelt concern, date, friendship (be better this time), love bucks (read this book as many times as needed), relationship, partner, counseling, marriage if you were not married, or remarriage if you are no longer married.

Slowly, carefully, patiently, and lovingly consummate when she is ready if both of you are able. Continue with a happy life again. How long will it take? I don't know how badly you messed up. I don't know how often you will mess up. Do you have to restart? It may be the only way. How often? As often as you want to or have to. I recommend restarting to many Christian brothers. There was someone who had to restart every day. His beautiful wife had a problem where she could not remember her husband was her husband. He had to restart from the beginning every day. He was married to her for life.

I tried to always be attuned to my wife's wants and concerns. I was willing to choose to quickly restart. God restarted many times. A few examples include the revolt in heaven in which God the Father was victorious, the creation of the earth, Adam's original sin, the first sacrificial lamb, Noah, Abraham, Moses, and Jesus.

Has the Father restarted for you? Has Jesus restarted for you? Take up thy cross and love.

> Husbands, love your wives even as Christ also
> loved the church and gave himself for it.
> —Ephesians 5:25 King James Version of Bible

So ought men to love their wives as their own bodies.
He that loveth his wife loveth himself.
—Ephesians 5:28 King James Version of Bible

Husbands, love your wives, and be not bitter against them.
—Colossians 3:19 King James Version of Bible

Christian values help make a good husband.

> By pureness, by knowledge, by long-suffering, by
> kindness, by the Holy Ghost, by love unfeigned.
> —2 Corinthians 6:6 King James Version of Bible

Can a good marriage be found by the fruit of the Spirit?

But the fruit of the Spirit is love, joy, peace,
longsuffering, gentleness, goodness, faith, meekness,
temperance: against such there is no law.
—Galatians 5:22–23 King James Version of Bible

Controlling your tongue is important in a marriage, and the subject can be a whole book by itself. It is important to choose your words wisely, especially when you are angry. In general, positive words will return positive words, and negative words will return negative words. Your tongue used loosely will set on fire the course of your marriage, but your precise, positive persistence will be an example for the house (James 3:6, 9–13).

Consider controlling and stifling unnecessary marital
arguments by responding to insults with blessings.
—1 Peter 3:9

Have you tried this yet?

Jesus is quoted in the New Testament saying the word "paradise."

Can you reconstruct what is required for paradise?

A definition of paradise is found in Genesis 2:21–25. Understand that before the fall, paradise and perfection did exist. No sin was committed by man or woman until the fall. The time before the fall was not written, but the experience is.

Paradise lost comes after the fall.

- Presence and access to our Creator: the true, alive permanent Being.
- Eternal day. God is light. There is not even a shadow. There are no morning or evening stars.
- Perfect weather and temperature, which we don't get now.
- One naked male and one naked female revealing their light within (good), demonstrating love to each other, and having no knowledge of their nakedness.
- The Messiah's example demonstrates how humans can defuse their darkness within (eliminating the darkness and the evil) and choose to bring their light within out to be shown. Light shown results in love, and there are no shadows.
- The Holy Spirit.
- Dressing and keeping a garden that is already perfect with animals at rest.

Sounds like a light burden!

The scriptures contain examples of good, which is often referred to as light. In addition to the figurative meaning, light can be understood literally as light. The word light can be found inside yourself. Biblically, it is called your heart. Light is worth seeking, struggling for, and asking for. It is somewhere deep inside you. Jesus, the Light of the world, spoke of taking the light from within you and placing it high to be seen. The light in you is worthy of being seen.

Make an effort to share the light within you with your bride often.

What God Wants to Hear Most

- questions asking to be surrounded in the light
- questions asking what God wants
- questions asking how God feels
- questions seeking God's face

He wants to hear you say the sign of the times statement, especially in Jerusalem: "Blessed is he that cometh (who comes) in the name of the Lord" (Matthew 23:39 King James Version of Bible).

Note that Job understood how words can be
used to strengthen and weaken with.
—Job 16:4

And the Lord heard it. If you have a problem, our
Lord listens, even to your grumbling!
—Numbers 12:2 King James Version of Bible

What will ye that I shall do unto you?
—Matthew 20:32 King James Version of Bible

Jesus asks the ultimate question that God, your parents, your wife, your children, and other people want to hear: "What do you want?"

The prodigal son could have been a true story experienced by many people, including myself. Have you personally experienced it? Upon completion of your unsafe journey in this world, God Almighty will run to you, take you in His arms with forgiveness, and say, "I love you!" Come back to Him. While you are living on this earth, will you forgive your wife and your children?

Whoso findeth a wife findeth a good thing,
and obtaineth favour of the Lord.
—Proverbs 18:22 King James Version of Bible

He who finds a wife obtains the Lord's gift. In the beginning, the women were the seekers and proposers. She who finds a husband obtains the Lord's gift. The person who finds the Lord keeps the Lord's gifts.

One Commandment

My summation of God's commandments, the true stories contained in His book, including the Old Testament and the New Testament: Man, awaken and show your love for God. Show Me you are capable of loving one woman and your children for life—your most important neighbors—and I will show you paradise!

It can't be made any easier!

CONCLUSION

Bear ye one another's burdens, and so fulfill the law of Christ.
—Galatian 6:2

This book tries to solve the problem God has been working on for lifetimes since the fall of man. It is the main problem Christ solves with His death on the cross and resurrection from the cave. Reconnecting us with God and neighbors. Understanding that our wives are our most important neighbor. My brothers and sisters, you were chosen to be free (Galatians 5: 13). Don't use your freedom as an excuse to live in sin. Instead, serve one another in love. The New International Reader's Version (NIRV) is used because sin can cover more than the flesh in today's marriages.

Getting the husband and wife to serve one another in love is putting very complicated bodies, spirits, and souls back together. You need a place to start. This book is for Christian men who have read the Bible, and like our Father and Son, it starts with the men. It teaches them how to pursue and love their wives like the Father and the Son pursue and love us. If a Christlike husband loves and pursues his wife—like Christ loves and pursues the church—it will be hard for the wife not to desire him, not to appreciate him, and not to love him for life.

This book contains a simplified version of what the Bible reveals as God's pursuit of love. What God has put together let no man separate!

Jesus is the Way, the Truth, and the Life!

No one comes to the Father but by Him!

Through Jesus, I can see!

NOTES

NOTES

NOTES

The Messiah is coming!

SpiritualFoodPublications.com

Spiritual Food Publications Corp.
P.O. Box 780197
Maspeth, NY 11378-9997
Order information:
Please send the following book: *How to Pick Your Bride and How to Keep Her for Life*
Name: _____
Address: _____
City: _____ State: _____ Zip: _____
Number of books buying _____
Please add 8.25 percent sales tax for books shipped to New York state addresses _____
Shipping:
Book Rate: $<u>12.95</u>
Total: $_____
(Surface shipping may take three to four weeks)
Payment:
[ ] Check
[ ] Credit Card:
Name: _____ Phone: _____
Card Number: _____
Expiration Date: _____
Card Verification Number _____

Printed in the United States
by Baker & Taylor Publisher Services